# THINKING OF YOU

# OF YOU

## (BUT NOT LIKE IN A WEIRD CREEPY WAY)

### beth evans

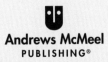

Andrews McMeel
PUBLISHING®

Andrews McMeel Publishing
a division of Andrews McMeel Universal
1130 Walnut Street, Kansas City, Missouri 64106

www.andrewsmcmeel.com

23 24 25 26 27 CHJ 10 9 8 7 6 5 4 3 2 1

ISBN: 978-1-5248-7978-5

Library of Congress Control Number: 2022946578

Editor: Patty Rice
Art Director: Tiffany Meairs
Production Editor: Jasmine Lim
Production Manager: Chadd Keim

# HI THERE!

## Welcome to the book!

I'm Beth. I like making comics that help people feel—sometimes it's helping them feel good or feel seen, and sometimes it hits a nerve someone didn't know they had. Most of all, I like to provide comfort, like a hug, when you really need one. Basically, even though we may not know each other, I'm here for you.

Providing support is something that comes naturally to me. I like caring about people and helping when things are hard. I might not always have the right thing to say, but I'll listen. And I like to think my comics do the same thing— they're the other end of a conversation you wish you could have.

Throughout this book, you'll find work on everyday anxieties, tough feelings, a helping hand when you could use one, and your own personal cheering section through it all. Things can be harder than people will ever know, especially when you need to be strong for everyone else around you (I know this feeling all too well). Here you'll find acknowledgment of those struggles but also that you're trying.

Trying is hard because you feel the need to prove to everyone around you that you are—*look at me! I'm trying! I've got this!* I think we often try in our daily lives by being friends, lending a helping hand when needed, and trying to do some good in the world. I know I'm really trying with this book. I want to create nice things for people.

So basically, welcome. I'm really glad you're here and that you took the time to read this. I hope you'll find something that helps along the way. I like to think I did too.

# EVERYDAY STRUGGLES

There is this fine line between things that are difficult in our everyday lives and outright disasters. And wow, can that line be fine!

Those little things in our everyday lives, from pesky emails to being afraid to open text messages, can feel like the end of the world. They mix in with the anxiety and dread we already have about the big stuff in life and compound into the worst elixir we continuously consume. By focusing on the little challenges to distract from the overwhelming stuff, they turn into the biggest worries ever.

You're not alone in trying to pull yourself out of this cycle. Your inbox pinging isn't going to cause everything to crash, and the new message icon on your phone truly isn't the end of the world, even if it very much feels like it. Getting through the days is hard—maybe even one of the harder parts of being human that we don't talk about. You're navigating and doing the best you can.

I sincerely hope the days get a little easier. You absolutely deserve it!

# Second guessing everything?

Take this comic as a sign to go for the plunge! Send that email, fire off a text - the sense of relief from simply doing is so worth it (hey, just like you!)

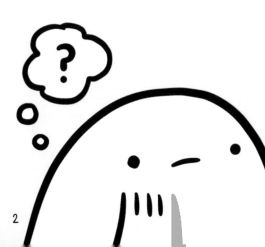

I KNOW NOT EVERY DAY IS GOING TO BE MY DAY, BUT IT WOULD BE NICE TO HAVE LIKE... AN HOUR

really, my best talent is having a perfectly good night out with friends and just overthinking everything I said and did to the extreme that I am convinced I only have enemies now

No one who worried about
not doing enough ever did
too little

Burnout can make you feel like you're never doing enough— but you're doing more than you realize— and a great job despite the pressures

There's this really awful feeling that you're running out of time for EVERYTHING

to achieve goals, create and keep relationships - to be a whole person

It's a lot - but remember, you are doing A **LOT** too, and all your efforts are incredible

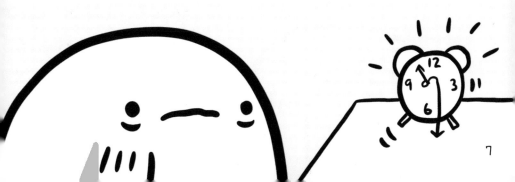

7

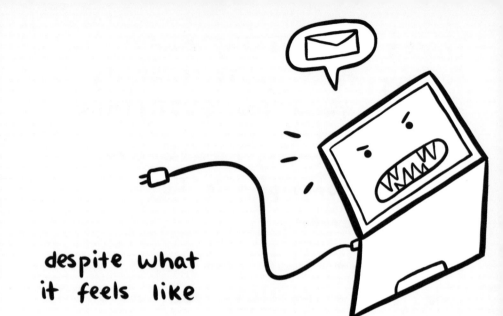

despite what
it feels like

that email in
your inbox you
are too afraid
to open won't
be the end of
the world

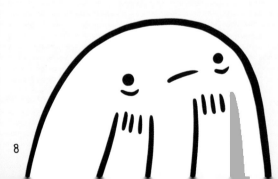

8

Progress can literally feel like walking around with a bar above us, desperate to prove to everyone we're getting there

You're doing just fine, promise!

NOW LOADING...

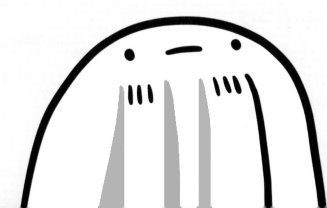

I'm just really
struggling with
my appearance
and perception—

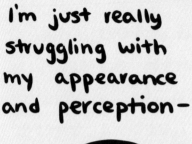

✳ have you
tried
self-love
✳

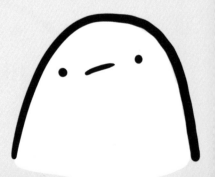

yep, that'll
undo the years
of trauma it's
based in

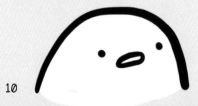

EMBARRASSING THING I DID YEARS AGO
lease, I'm so uch more ingey NOW

Do yourself a favor-
don't look up that
person you went to
school with, even if
stuff was kinda OK

You're needed here and
now – and matter here too

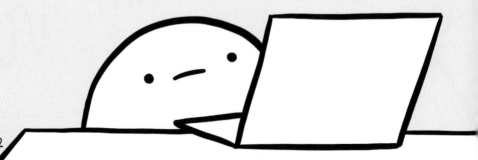

12

# HE "I SPENT MONEY" CYCLE

I need this
impulse purchase
or I will die

yay it's mine!

wait I spent
MONEY, this is
very bad

never again!
I will always
be smart with
money now!

13

Some problems can't be
solved on love - given to
us or through ourselves

It's okay if your problems
don't have a perfectly
lovely solution

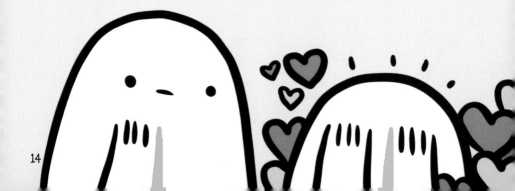

14

# TODAY'S PANIC DOES NOT HAVE TO BE TOMORROW'S PROBLEM

It can be scary and all consuming - but even if you struggle to control your panic, just know you are so much more than it ♡

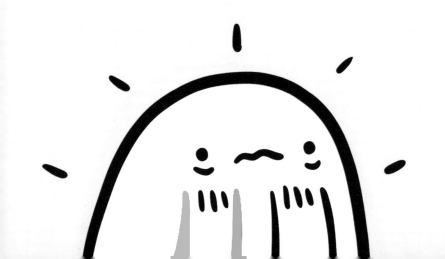

thank you for being here
and for being you
and for all that you do ♡

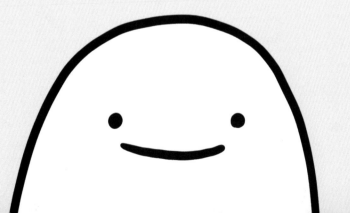

DESPITE WHAT YOU
MIGHT THINK, THAT
EMAIL OR TEXT YOU
ARE AFRAID TO OPEN
CANNOT MAGICALLY
KILL YOU OR ANYTHING

Just making it from one day to another is really great –

just like you!

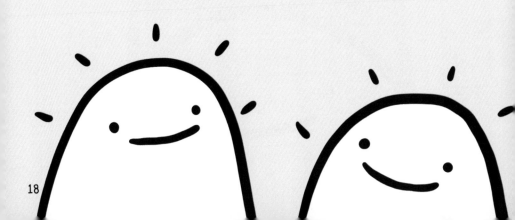

Sometimes you have no one in your corner and you need to figure out how to pick yourself up again and again

It's tough, and you're doing your best with it – I'm offering my support to you

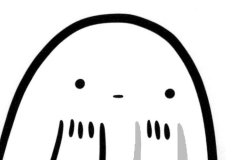

19

It can often feel like you're the only person ever who doesn't have it together - like everyone else knows exactly what they're doing, and you're the only one who doesn't

you're not alone in just trying to figure it all out, no matter your age or stage in life

UHHH

some people
can be friendly

some people
can be friends

some people are
not interested in
mixing the two

it's a tough
lesson to learn-
but you do deserve
people who care
about you

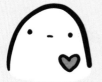

21

you may feel awful —

but you're still awfully great to me

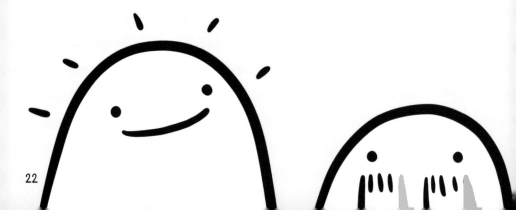

what's going on how's
work how's life are you
in a relationship—

23

be confident and love yourself, those are qualities people _LIKE_

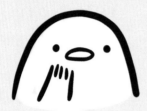

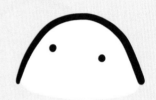

uhhh I CAN DO THIS and ummmmm I AM GREAT ew this is exhausting—

≥sniff≥ beautiful!

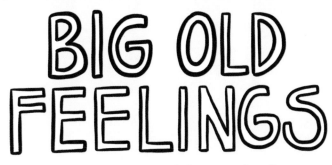

# BIG OLD FEELINGS

Sometimes everything is simply too much for you to handle.

I just wanted to let you know you are so much more than what you are feeling right now. You are a person, first and foremost—a person who has thoughts and interests and likes and dislikes and a whole worldview. You are so much more than the problems at hand and all the things that are crushing your spirit.

And I think you are great.

Getting through these tough times when you feel so fragile sucks. It's not easy. You have to dig deep in that internal part of yourself and pull out all the energy you can to power through everything at hand. That takes guts and is very brave of you. You are rising and meeting the challenges life throws at you day after day. It might not look like a loud, bold charge at handling things, but the quiet pushing ahead is just as important.

I know it's really difficult to keep steady and keep moving forward. Just know that even though we don't know each other personally, I am cheering for you. I want nothing but good things for you. I'm out there in the world, just like you, trying to do my best, and I know you are too.

25

Whenever your brain
tells you THIS

oh, it's lying

despite what you think, you
aren't the worst ever —
you're just a person with
a rude brain

Sometimes it feels like you're just a vessel for big, overwhelming, too-much-to-deal-with feelings

you've got a lot of other qualities in there too that help quiet that oh-so-loud spiral, and they matter too - like you!

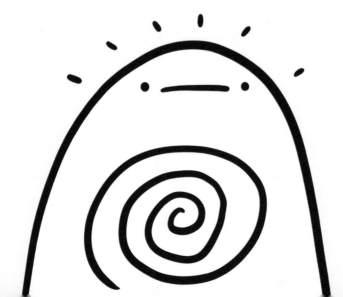

It's easy to fall into a shame spiral, but harder to believe you're a pretty great person (hint: you are!)

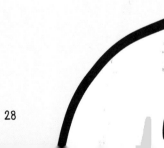

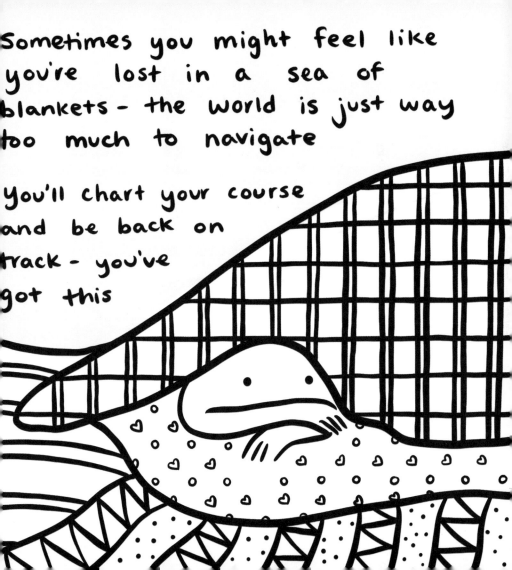

Sometimes you might feel like you're lost in a sea of blankets - the world is just way too much to navigate

You'll chart your course and be back on track - you've got this

you don't have to
untangle it all today

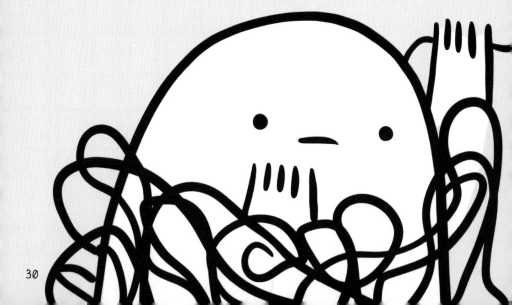

**CYCLE**
**OF**
**THOUGHTS**

it's just
a
thought...

...NO it's my entire
reality going forward
and it's awful and I'm
awful and—

oh wow
look
something
NEW
to be
upset
about!

Even when you feel lost in the clouds, you still deserve all the sunny days

This isn't going to last forever ♡

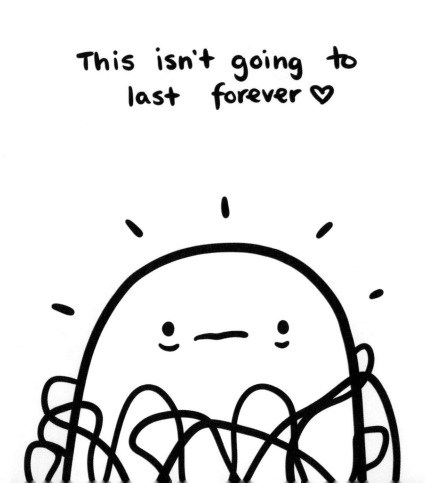

Sometimes we dig deep to help others feel better when we ourselves aren't doing too great either

It's a lot, but also a huge gift to give - you're phenomenal

Whatever you're feeling,
it doesn't mean you don't
deserve all the love ♡

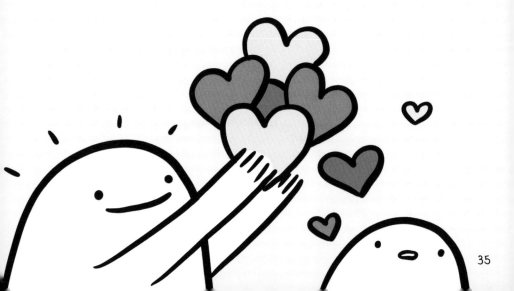

35

Feelings are weird and don't always make sense

It's OK, you're dealing with them the best you can

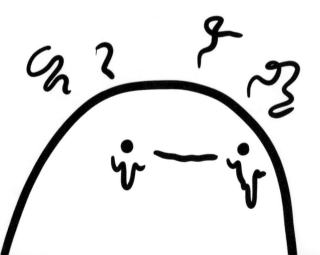

Panic spirals happen

you've survived them before and
you can survive this one now

Here's to unwinding soon!

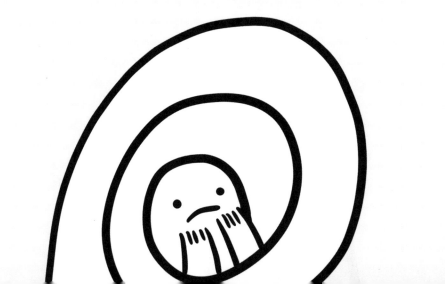

Sometimes our worry makes us feel silly - like hey, who would even worry about this but <u>ME?</u>

Your worry may be difficult, but it does show you care

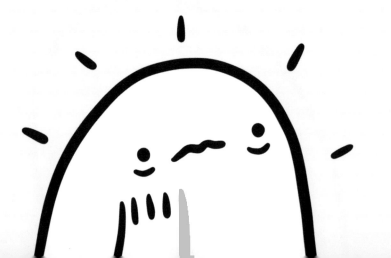

TODAY MIGHT FEEL LIKE THE END OF THE WORLD (AND THAT'S KIND OF SCARY) BUT STICK AROUND AND SEE WHAT TOMORROW IS ANYWAY ♡

stress may occupy a big
place in your life -

but you're <u>so</u> much more
than one icky feeling

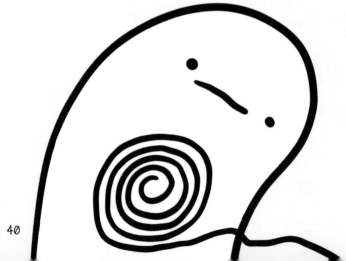

You know when stuff has been so bad for so long you're too afraid to even enjoy good stuff when it happens?

Indulge a little, you definitely deserve it!

41

# ONE LITTLE THING GOES WRONG

well I'm taking this personally and assuming everything is going to hell

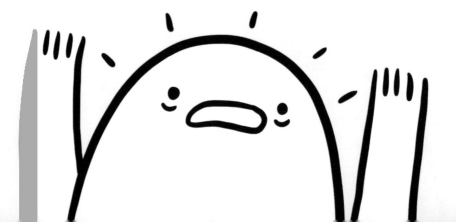

THIS FEELING WILL NOT LAST FOREVER AND NEITHER WILL WHAT'S GOING ON RIGHT NOW

Unfortunately you can't make people want to be a part of your life, no matter how badly you want them there

It's tempting to blame yourself entirely, but relationships are two ways - and if you are reflecting, you've likely done all you can

Things ache, hurt, and feel totally upside down right now

But things also have a chance to flip over and send you the right direction – stay the course, you've totally got this

45

spinning the wheel of worry?



OVER-COMMITTED TO TOO MUCH AND I DON'T WANNA DO ANY OF IT!
MY WHOLE APPEARANCE
IF WORK AND GETTING I'M, LIKE, ANYWHERE IN LIFE
FRIENDSHIPS RELATIONSHIPS AND ALL SOCIAL THINGS- AHHH
IDK I JUST DON'T LIKE MYSELF!!!
TIME PASSING BY, AND I AM DOING NOTHING
AM I A GOOD PERSON OR THE WORST EVER?!?
#IAMOVERPARTY
A BUNCH OF MADE UP SCENARIOS IN MY HEAD THAT SUCK


it's ok-
you're doing
your best ♡

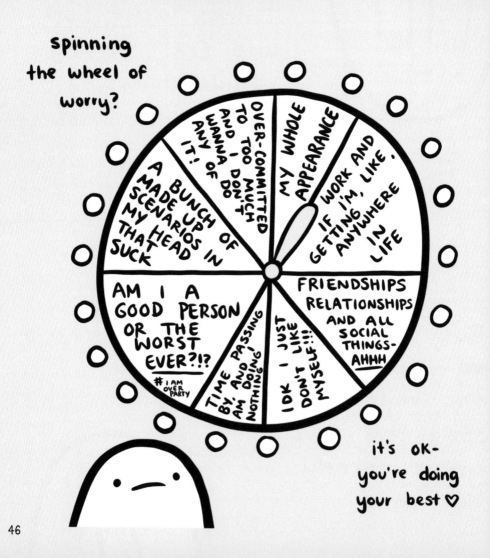

sometimes all you can do is hang on
oh wow
MY LIFE IS GOING DOWNHILL

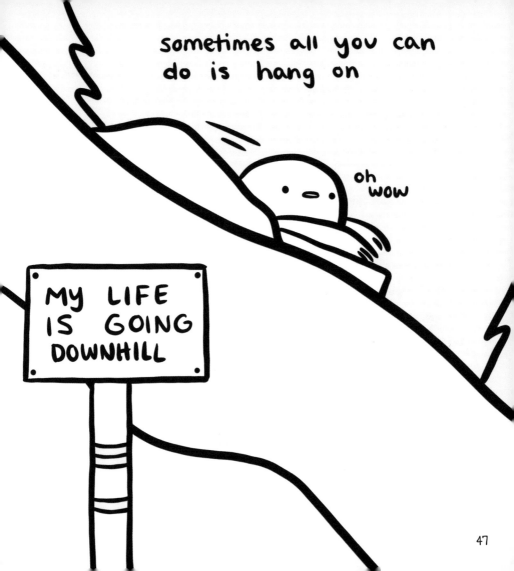

I know it's good to stay positive and all that

but it doesn't match what I'm experiencing, which is Bad Stuff All At Once

like every day I get more bad news and I'm just trying to deal with it, so being told to just look at the good when it's non-existant is hard

I think it's OK to feel what you're feeling right now, especially during challenging times like these - it's OK to feel stuff

# GO YOU!!!

Okay, team! Let's talk.

It might seem like life has us beaten at this point.

I know, I know, the score seems ridiculous, and life keeps pulling out all these different tricks we didn't even know or see coming. That additional stressor we didn't even know about totally delayed us when we wanted to succeed, and the relationship ending certainly complicated things. It's been a tough fight.

But we have *heart*.

We have soul. We have the courage to keep getting up when we're knocked down. And darn it, we keep getting up! Look at how we thought that problem was world-ending—it didn't stop us yet. And we totally made it through all that family drama. Our hearts and souls keep us pumping and keep us going, and we keep on going.

Look at us. We can do this. But most importantly, I know you can do this. Your talent, humor, personality, kindness, and awareness of the world will take you places. I know it seems like we're down at the buzzer, but we can do this.

*You can do this.*

Go you!!!

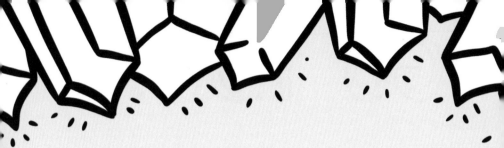

you shine brighter than
you even know

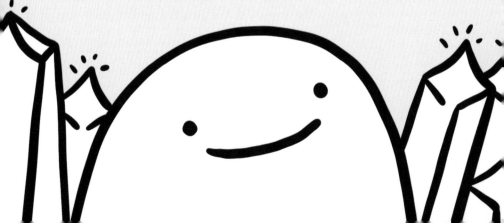

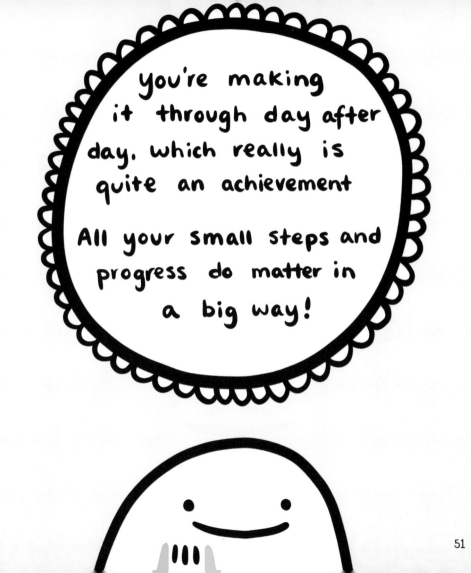

you're making it through day after day, which really is quite an achievement

All your small steps and progress do matter in a big way!

51

you deserve nothing but
the fullest bloom life has
to    offer ❀

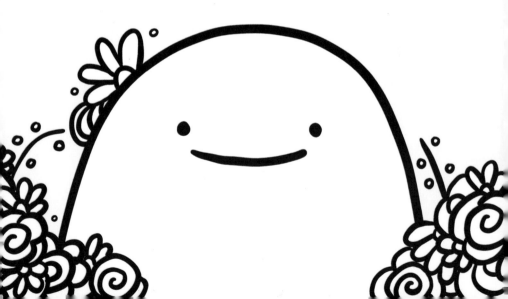

You're doing better than you
even know just by being you

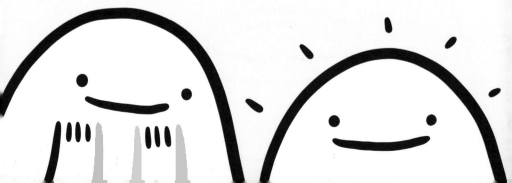

proud of your progress—
all of it!

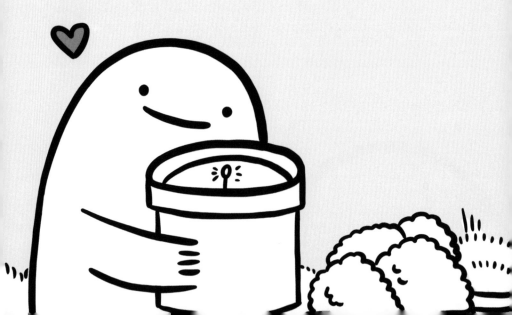

YOU'VE TOTALLY
GOT THIS
EVEN IF IT DOESN'T
FEEL LIKE IT

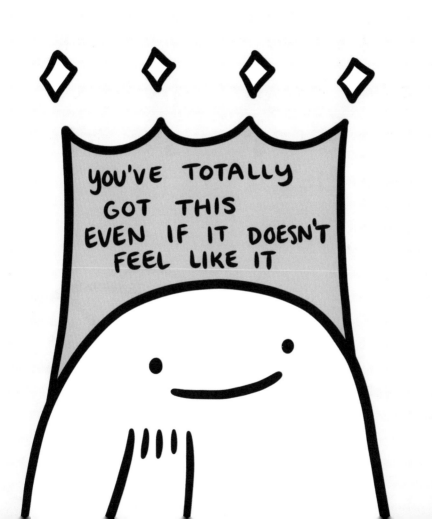

you never know what
new heights growth
and change might take
you to

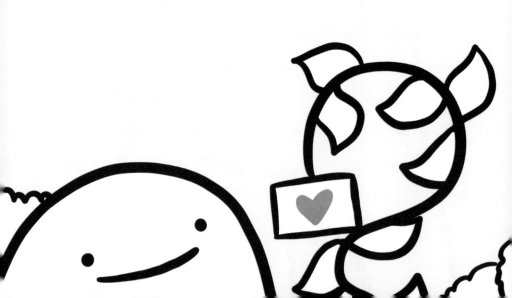

your bloom, no matter
how small, matters too

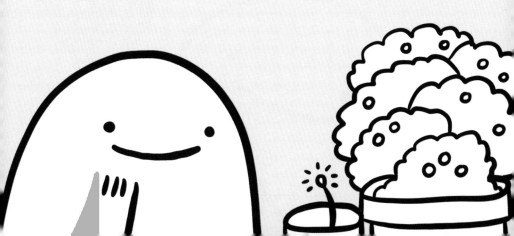

don't be afraid
to let your heart
be your guide

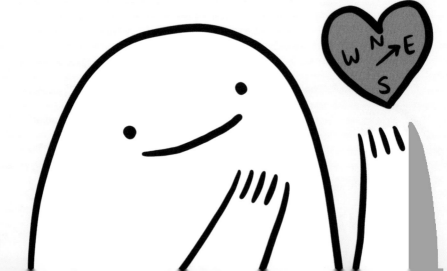

Here's hoping something
nice comes your way
(you deserve it!)

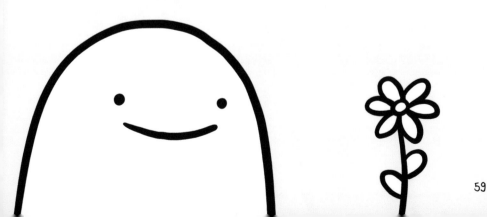

ALL THAT EVERY DAY STUFF YOU DO DOES MATTER (AND SO DO YOU!)

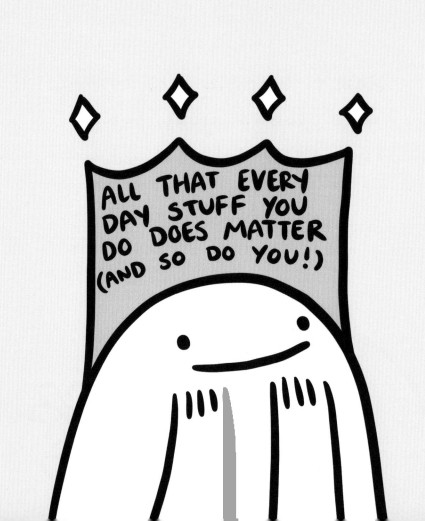

YOU DON'T NEED TO BE ANYTHING MORE THAN YOU ALREADY ARE SINCE YOU'RE AWESOME

One step at a time
you're doing just fine

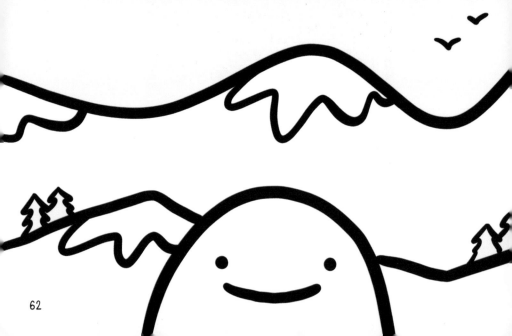

keep going
keep doing
keep trying
keep being you

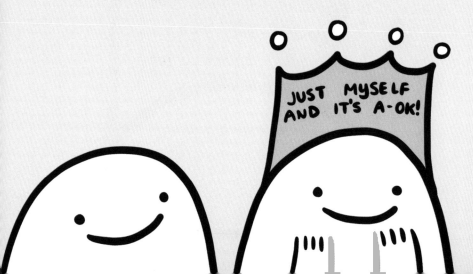

ONE STEP AT A TIME, YOU'RE DOING JUST FINE

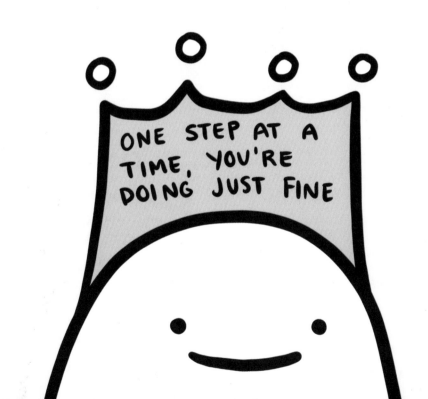

Even if you're moving at a snail's pace, you're still moving

Every step, no matter how small or slow, is cheer worthy

YOU?
MAKING IT
THROUGH

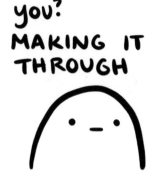

YOUR EFFORT?
ABSOLUTELY
AMAZING

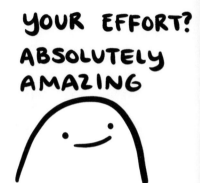

YOU STILL
DOING STUFF
EVEN WHEN
STUFF SUCKS?
ASTOUNDING!

YOU?

PRETTY
DARN GREAT♡

It may not always feel
like it – but you can do this

you <u>can</u> get through all of this

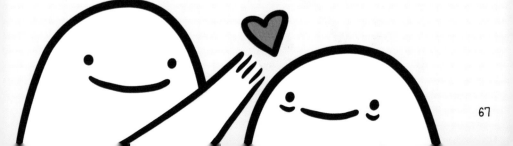

Look at you, still getting through stuff even when it feels like you're going to throw up!

That takes guts - especially when you feel like you've lost yours

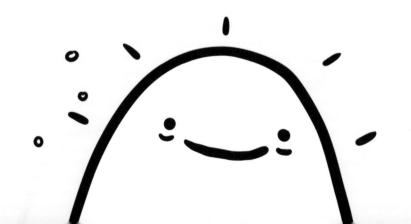

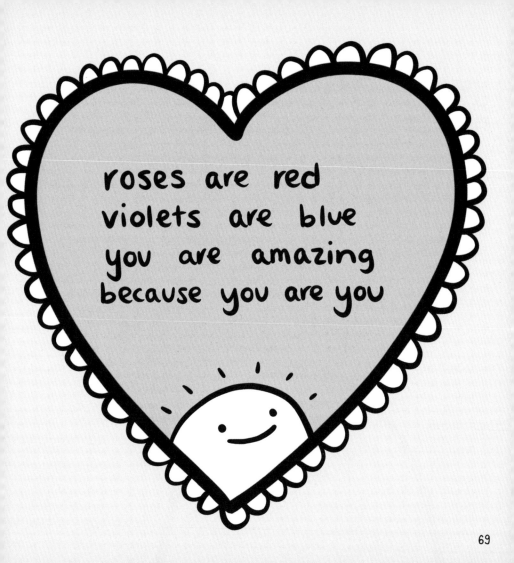

roses are red
violets are blue
you are amazing
because you are you

69

you do deserve all the nice things, no matter what your brain tells you otherwise

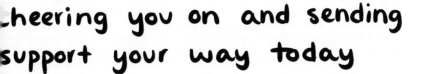

cheering you on and sending
support your way today

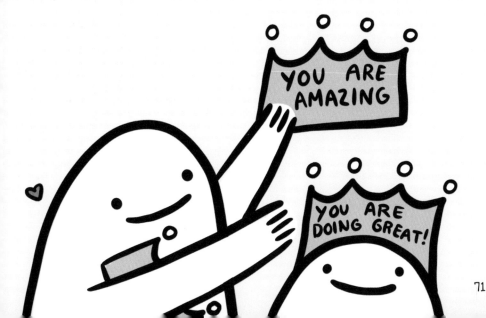

71

psst...
stuff might suck, but I hope this page is a little kinder to you ♥

# HARD THINGS AND VALIDATION

Sometimes things suck. And sometimes, they're really bad for a really long time.

These hard times can be such a challenge to keep pushing through. Motivation can be lost, and any kind of goal waiting for you might be non-existent. To keep picking yourself up over and over again and try? That's amazing. And you are amazing.

I genuinely believe everyone deserves nice things. This sounds like a blanket statement, but I think it's important. Sometimes our minds trick us and push us down, convincing us that we don't deserve much of anything. But I think we do deserve good stuff in life. Maybe it's friends, a bit of good luck, or a push forward in the right direction—everyone should get a chance at things that feel good. Especially you, reader. No matter what your brain says, I promise it's lying. You do deserve the good things.

Basically, I know life is all about the journey, etc. But no one tells you how long or how hard that road will be—or just how tired you might get on it. Just know I'm walking next to you, putting my best foot forward too, and just hoping for the best, even though I don't always know what I'm doing.

You're not alone in it. I see how hard you're trying. You'll always have a friend in me.

Sometimes stress is an
overwhelming beast to try
to tame - and when it stops
by on a daily basis, it can
be way too much to handle

You're balancing a lot
and doing the best you
can right now - take a
deep breath before you
face it all again

you're
doing
just
fine

74

you don't have to be the most perfect climber of mountains when big challenges are placed in front of you

you're facing stuff, and that's a pretty big feat to scale in itself

A really sucky time can feel like it will last forever

Things will change and be un-stuck - they might not change how we want them to, and it might be difficult -

but this moment now won't last forever

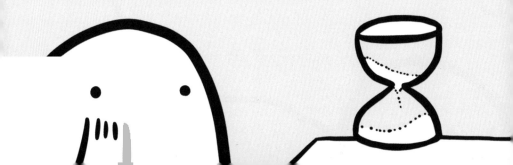

you're doing the best you can to face challenges each day - that's a fantastic accomplishment, and you're pretty fantastic too!

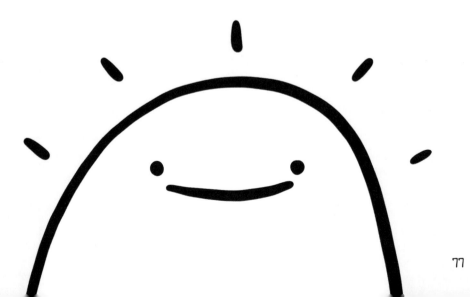

We don't always know what the road we're on will bring, but moving forward is a total achievement in itself - wherever you end up, you'll do great

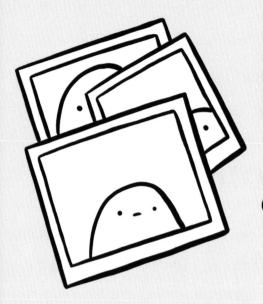

Sometimes we want to crawl back to times in our lives - even if they weren't that happy or great (it's a weird feeling!)

It's OK to be open to other times that you might want to mentally capture and pine for one day too

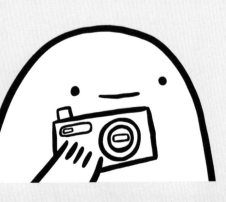

It's OK if you don't exactly know how to deal with things perfectly and you're constantly asking "HOW DO I EVEN GET THROUGH THIS?!?"

One step at a time- you can get through this, and I'll be cheering you on

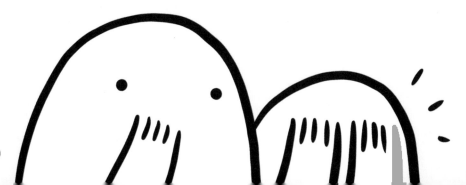

There can be this huge pressure to be warm and funny and totally personable, and we feel like we aren't measuring up to all these huge perfect human expectations

Whatever you're worried you're really like - you're pretty great

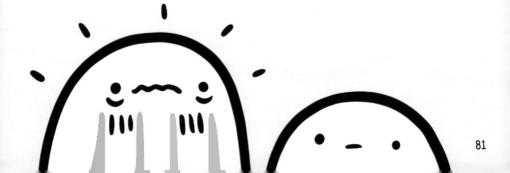

Sometimes you feel so adrift, like everything will be choppy waters forever and ever

You do deserve smooth sailing - you'll get there in time

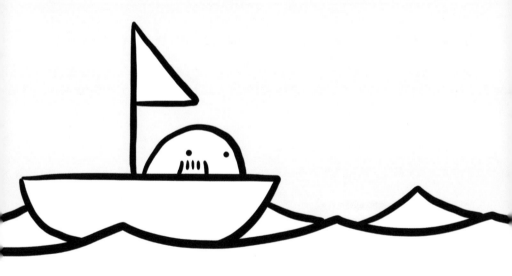

you shine brighter than
you even know

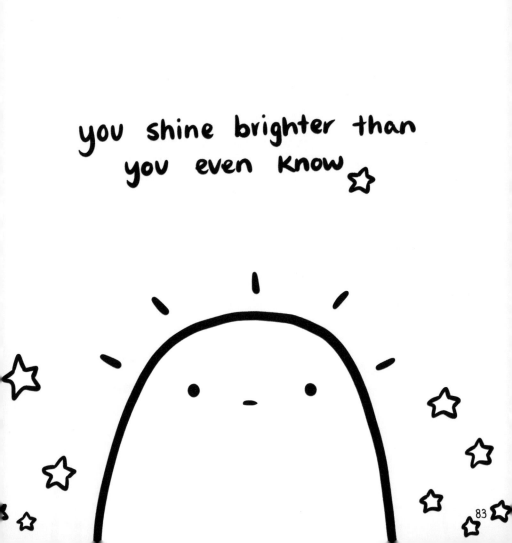

Sometimes we don't have the right words for what we're going through

Sometimes others don't have the right words to help us

It's always appreciated just being there

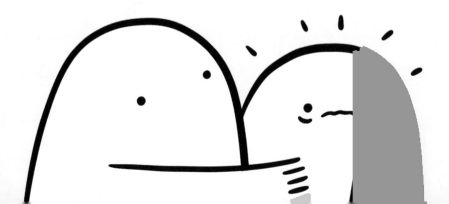

Sometimes, everything doesn't work out OK, no matter how positive our attitude is

And that's OK

Everything can't be fixed or healed, and we do our best to cope with that, and it's OK

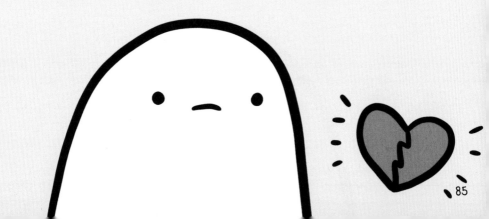

85

you know when people are like "everything will be okay" and you know things won't be for you?

It's hard

You're doing the best you can with impossible situations

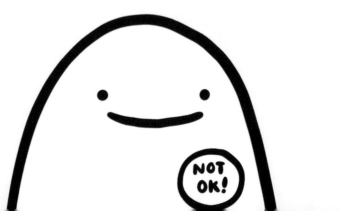

Sometimes failure can feel like a one person pit of despair

Keep treading, keep trying - you're going to make it out of that pit


WELCOME TO
DESPAIR
POPULATION: YOU

sometimes when you're always the "strong" person, people really struggle if you show any kind of vulnerability or pain

it takes strength to show those too, especially when everyone expects you to have it all together

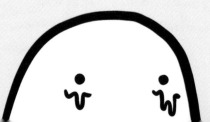

When you're everyone's emotional support system, it can be so hard when people expect you to endlessly give, and that you never need any support yourself

It's okay to take a step back and focus on supporting y<u>ou</u>

You matter too

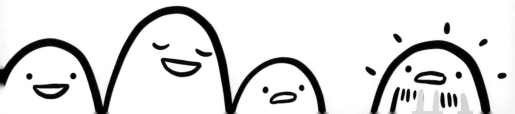

Messes and accidents happen

You'll figure out how to clean up and move ahead - you've got this

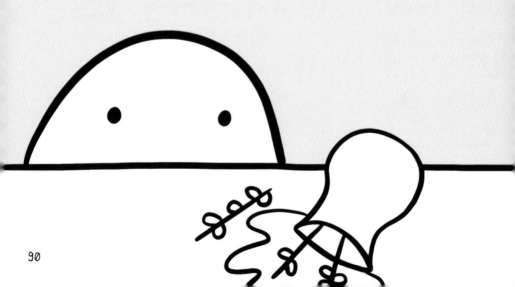

take your time
you're doing the best you can
it's OK not to do it all today
you're doing a great job- better than you even know
you're gonna get through this time- you can do it
because you're you- and that is so awesome
you've got this ♡

# CERTIFICATE OF GETTING THROUGH STUFF

This hereby certifies that_____
is ~~totally~~ getting through some
really big stuff and it's not
always easy - but it's an
accomplishment all the same!

_____
(your name - yes you!)

beth evans
_____
(me, cheering you on)

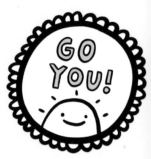

When we're younger, people find ways to throw insults and be really hurtful

As adults, people find ways to repackage and do the same things

It's OK to still be affected and not perfectly "rise above" every time someone is awful to you

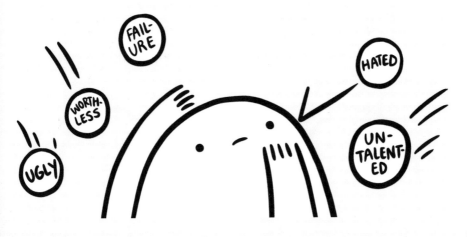

things are
rough

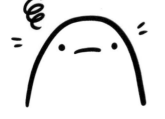

but you're
getting
through the
days

your heart is in
the right place
and you're trying
your best

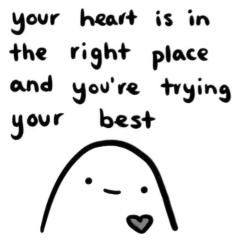

you really
are quite
remarkable!

It might not feel like you can get through these tough times right now

But you've survived so many already – and you can get through this too

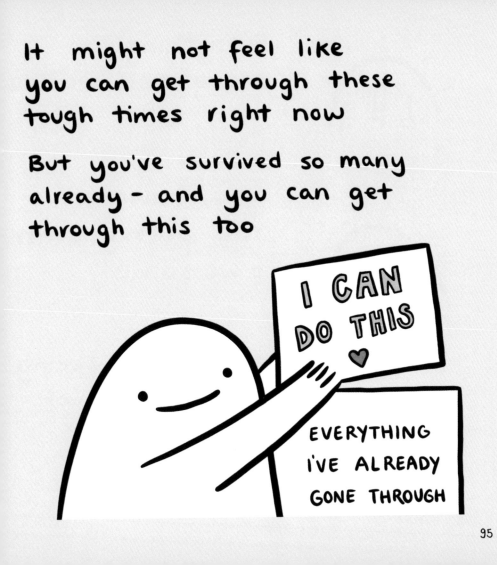

 Everything is
scary and terrible.

 You, however,
are pretty darn
awesome

 Thanks for facing
another day of
all of this -
you're doing
great ♡

# UPLIFTING MESSAGES

This is the "you're doing just fine" section.

Now, it might not necessarily feel like it. In fact, it might feel like your world is spinning out of control at a thousand miles an hour, everything is a complete and total mess, and there seems to be no path forward. And some stranger in a book is going to tell you *you're doing just fine*?

Yes.

I sincerely believe being human is one of the biggest and hardest things we can ask of people - and ourselves. There are so many different dynamics to it. So many feelings, thoughts, worries, fears, struggles, challenges, and horrible aspects to it. Every day that you're here and facing those things and choosing to stick around and do it all over again?

That takes bravery. That takes guts. And you have both.

So yes, I do think you're doing just fine, doing whatever it is that you do. You're human, and you're doing. There's not much more you can ask of yourself. I'm sending you a virtual hand squeeze if you need one, from one messy person to another.

Just because you're having a bad day doesn't mean you yourself are bad - today doesn't define all those lovely parts of you that make you, well - you!

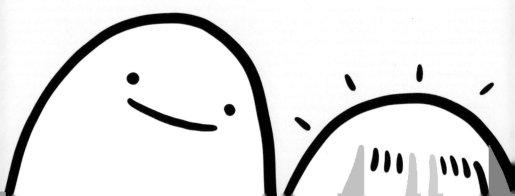

This might be the
WORST. DAY. EVER.

But this also might
not be forever

Hold steady, you're
doing great and can
get through this ♡

TAKING YOUR TIME
IS JUST FINE

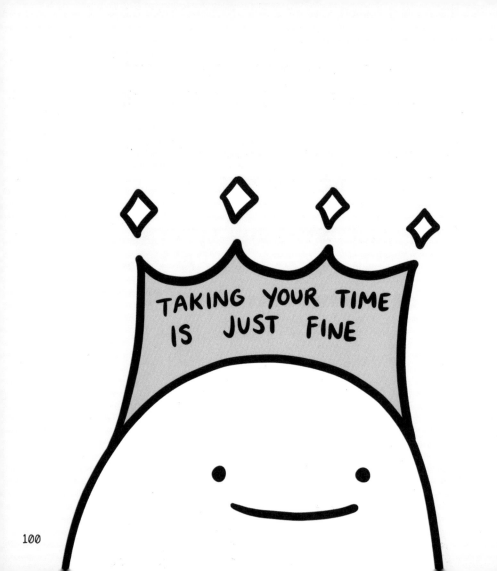

you don't have to be an amazing super human to successfully get through the day - you're doing just fine

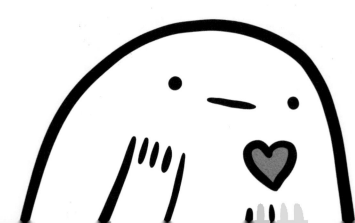

TOMORROW IS A CLEAN SLATE, AND YOU CAN REFRESH IT HOWEVER YOU WANT TO - YOU'VE TOTALLY GOT THIS!

A little love from
me to you-

just a reminder you're
oh-so-special

All the things that make you, well - you

They're awesome, unique, and should be celebrated, just like you!

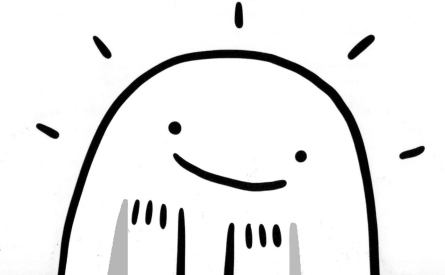

YOU'RE DOING BETTER THAN YOU EVEN KNOW

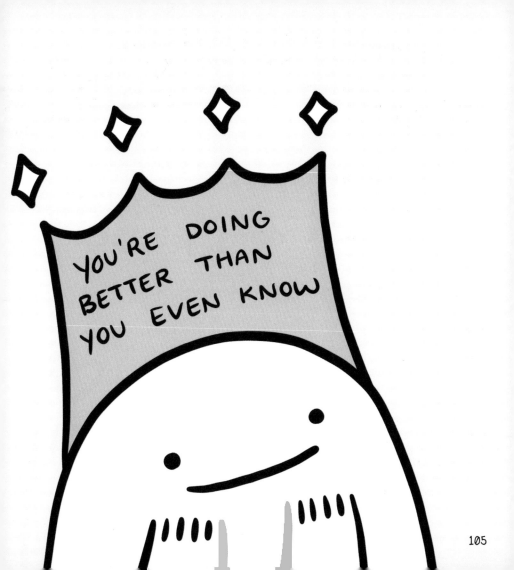

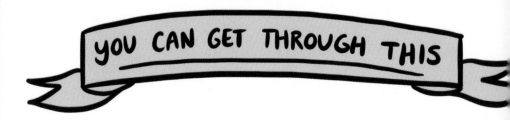

YOU CAN GET THROUGH THIS

Stuff sucks

You're doing your best

Keep at it

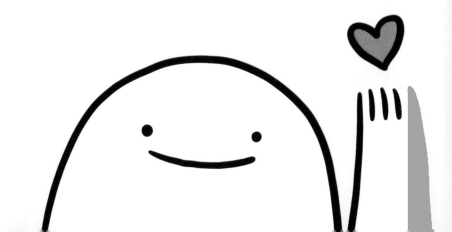

It may not always feel like it, but you are doing a really great job

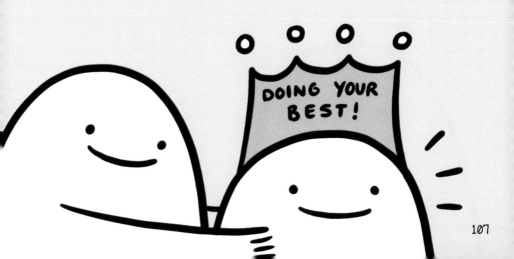

you don't have to be perfect to be absolutely perfect to someone - seeing the real you is an absolute privilege, and you're a real treasure

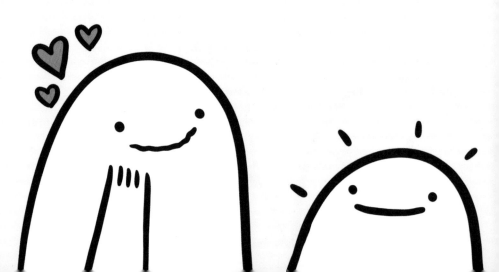

you've been through so much
already. I know you can
get through this too

you've got this

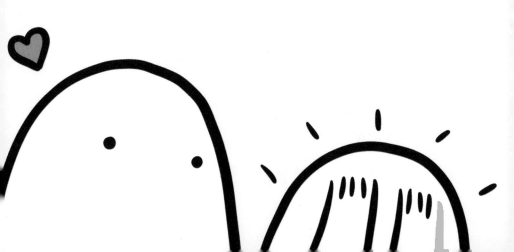

Strength doesn't mean "dealing with everything perfectly and unbothered"

Sometimes it's just getting through - go you!

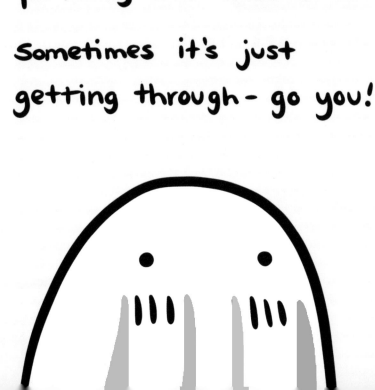

today?

it can't be worse
than yesterday

proud of you and all that
you face on a daily basis

you're doing great

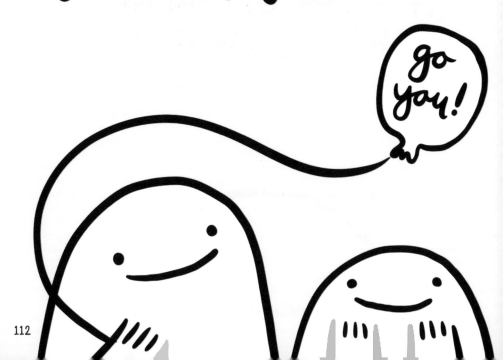

 yesterday's
panic?

 today's
anxieties?

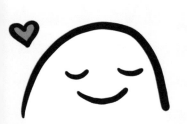 here's
hoping tomorrow
brings you some
level of peace

113

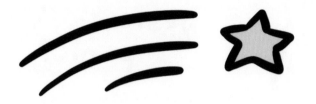

I hope something nice comes your way

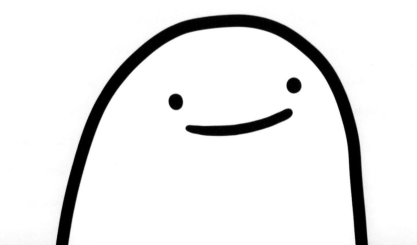

oh but you do deserve all the love!

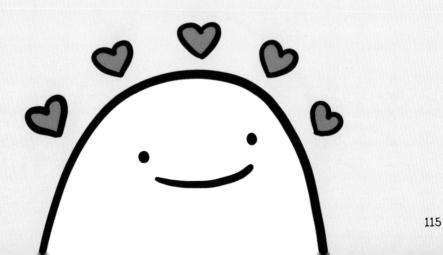

It might not feel like it, but -
# YOU CAN DO THIS
Tell yourself it anyway!

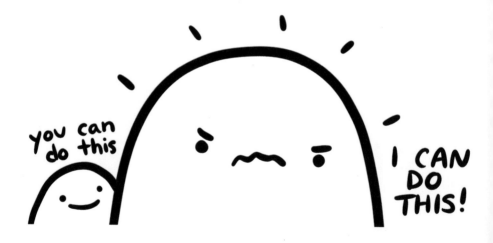

YOU DON'T HAVE TO DO IT ALL TODAY
YOUR OWN PACE IS FANTASTIC TOO - LIKE YOU

DOING YOUR BEST
DOING WHAT YOU CAN
DOING AMAZING!!!
GO YOU!

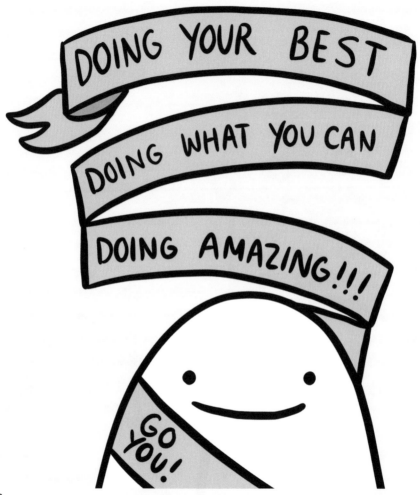

verything might be hard and
mpossible right now-

but you're following your
heart and trying your best,
and can't ask much more of
yourself than that!

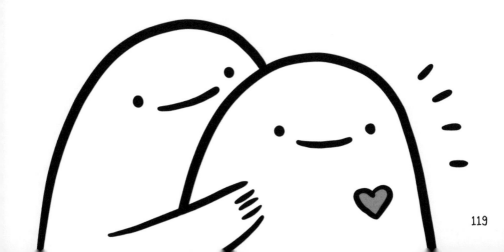

119

just because today
is bad

doesn't mean <u>you</u>
are bad

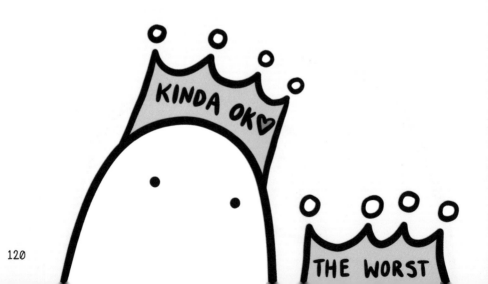

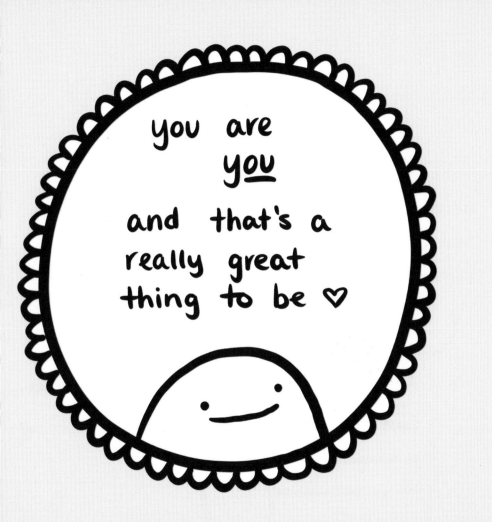

you are
<u>you</u>

and that's a
really great
thing to be ♡

I'm so tired of growing and changing. can't someone be happy I'm not dead yet
"grow" you!
dammit

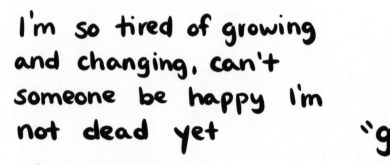

As long as I have a package to obsessively track, I can probably get through anything


bzzzt!

# ABOUT THE AUTHOR

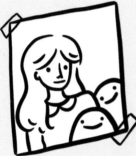

Hi! I'm Beth Evans. I make these blob friends that you have seen in this book.

I just wanted to tell you that I too have felt - and dealt with - a lot. It is not easy. Please know I am very much in your corner, and I am sending my love to you.

♡ beth